Contents

1

Winning and losing

Partnership

Desirable outcomes

The long-term view

What are my existing skills?
How can I become more effective?
What is my negotiating style?

Why do we need negotiating skills?

AT work do you ever
have to:
■ persuade
colleagues and team
members to prioritize
your projects or tasks?
■ make a case to
your manager for a
salary increase?
■ compete with
colleagues for a share
of resources such as
budgets or equipment?
■ seek out the best
deals on goods and
services?

Have you ever wondered why some people seem to be able to get what they want while others don't? Some people seem to have the knack of influencing people in such a way as to make it easy for them to cooperate. This is the skill of negotiating and it's growing in importance in the business world.

An increasingly important skill

Against the background of the "leaner" or "fitter" business, job roles are open to much wider interpretation, there is much tighter control on costs and you are more likely to come into direct contact with both customers and suppliers. Even internally, there is a greater need to negotiate with colleagues to achieve the desired standards and outcomes.

This has led to an increase in the demand for information about how to negotiate more effectively.

The costs of poor negotiation

Many people approach business negotiations with feelings of trepidation. The stakes can be high – especially if you get it wrong! You may worry about being tied into contracts that will cost you dear in the longer term.

Especially if you are inexperienced, you may come off badly in dealings with a professional negotiator. You could be pressurized into an agreement that does not meet your needs and that you will not be able to get out of.

Effective negotiation

Successful negotiation is an important communication skill, and only by mastering it can you increase your chances of gaining the outcomes that you want in your business life. Whether it is negotiating your salary or a large contract with a customer or supplier, the guidelines are the same.

■ You should reach the agreement that most nearly meets both your requirements.

■ Whatever the outcome of the discussion, you should have conducted the process in a professional way that reflects well on you – and your company, if you are representing them.

■ You should have laid a good foundation for any future dealings that you may need to have with the other person.

Outcomes

Although negotiations can take place in a vast variety of situations – in everyday life, at work, between individuals or teams of people – there are really only four possible outcomes, which are defined according to whether either or both parties achieves a satisfactory result. These are outlined below. The effective negotiator should always be aiming to achieve a WIN:WIN outcome.

I WIN: YOU LOSE

This is where you decide that, whatever the cost to the other person, you will go all out to get what you want. The end justifies the means. If you choose this approach you may win the battle but lose the war – the next time you have to deal with the other person they will feel that there is a score to be settled and so they will be much more difficult to deal with. This type of negotiator chooses to ignore the feelings of others.

I LOSE: YOU LOSE

If people have a very negative view of their position, they can decide to make other people's lives equally difficult and miserable. These people will actively seek out areas of disagreement and enjoy uncovering problems. They are often stuck in a very limited view of the world and will reject any creative solutions that could provide a way forward.

I LOSE: YOU WIN

If you go into any situation feeling that you have no chance of getting what you want, this can turn into a self-fulfilling prophecy. This state of mind produces poor performance and often acts as an excuse for people not even trying to be successful. It is sometimes referred to as the "victim" syndrome. Its proponents seem to distance themselves from any responsibility for the outcome.

I WIN: YOU WIN

Where both sides have an expectation of a successful outcome, they are more likely to make the effort to find reasonable solutions. Of course, this usually means that neither side will get everything they want but the areas on which they decide to compromise are viewed as being less important than finding some middle ground. Ideally the outcome will be one that offers advantages to both sides.

Start to improve your skills

This book is designed to help those who have to enter into business negotiations in a variety of situations. It provides tips and techniques that will ensure that you go into deals with your eyes open. It also aims to highlight a range of issues that must be addressed in order to prevent the reader falling into the obvious traps that can litter the path of successful negotiations.

In order to achieve this you need to develop an understanding of the process of negotiations and to identify a structure that will help you to navigate your way through the process. You should aim to increase your appreciation of the impact of your interpersonal skills and to be aware of some of the techniques, both positive and negative, that you will encounter in your dealings with others.

THINKING ABOUT NEGOTIATION

Try to remember some recent situations where you have had to negotiate with others. Don't just choose obvious situations, such as agreeing a contract at work. It could have been hiring a plumber, buying a car, agreeing a rota for domestic tasks at home, or asking your manager for a salary increase. Ask yourself the following questions about each one:

■ What was the outcome, and which of the four categories did it fall into?

■ To what extent did your initial view of the situation affect the outcome?

■ What do you think the other party's expectations were?

■ What did you learn from your experience?

■ What would you do differently next time?

What constitutes a negotiation?

A negotiation is the process whereby two parties reach an agreement for mutual benefit. For a negotiation to take place, certain conditions must exist.

- At least two parties are involved, but there may be more.
- Both parties must have something to gain from the negotiation. Both will have wants or needs, but also underlying interests that need to be met for the agreement to succeed.
- Both parties must have something to offer as well as something to gain. An employee asking his manager for a salary increase is merely making a request; if he can offer something in return, such as improved performance, then he is in a position to negotiate.
- Any obstacles to the final agreement must be overcome. Both sides involved in the negotiation will need to be prepared to compromise on some of the issues in order to reach agreement on the outcome.
- Both parties must have the authority to offer terms and agree to compromise. Alternatively, they must be in a position to confer with someone who has that authority.
- Both parties must want to reach an agreement. Sometimes when you are negotiating this will not seem to be the case – the other party might seem to be trying to sabotage the proceedings. (For advice on how to deal with these situations see Chapter Seven.)

NEGOTIATE – A DICTIONARY DEFINITION

- To bargain (with), to confer (with) for the purpose of coming to an agreement or arrangement.
- To arrange for by agreement (e.g. a treaty, a loan); to transfer or exchange for value (e.g. a bill, cheque); to get past (e.g. an obstacle, a difficulty).
- Negotiable (of bills, drafts, cheques etc.), capable of being transferred or assigned in the course of business from one person to another.

(Chambers Everyday Dictionary)

What skills do you already possess?

The first step towards improvement is to realize that negotiation is something you do all of the time. In everyday life you negotiate a whole number of issues. Parents strike bargains with their children ("I'll give you pocket money if you tidy your room"), while partners negotiate ways of living together ("I'll do the cooking if you do the gardening"). You buy and sell houses and cars. You agree to exchange your time for payment when you go to work and you enter into a variety of "contracts" with your bank, building society and other service providers, such as cleaners, builders, nannies, garages and electricians.

What makes a good negotiator?

The difference between a good and a bad negotiator, whether in business or in daily life, is that the former has thought about what they are doing, has prepared thoroughly, and has taken the time to think through the situation from the other person's point of view. They have considered what factors could hinder the process and tried to think of ways around problem areas.

Taking on a builder

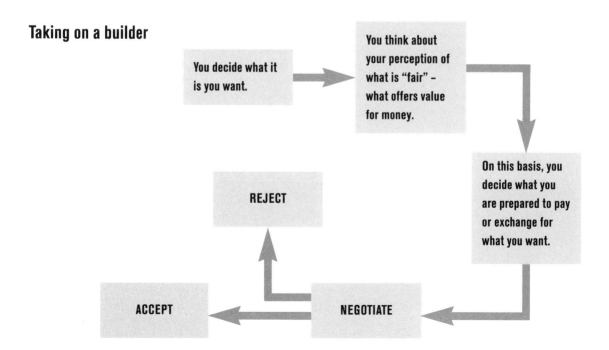

A positive approach

When you are fully prepared, you are able to negotiate from a position of strength. You will feel, and appear to be, more confident and assertive in your dealings with others. If you go into a situation believing that there is a high chance of success, this enables you to deal with other people in a positive way. The ineffective negotiator enters the negotiations unprepared, appears less organized and less confident, and so is less likely to achieve the outcome they desire.

"Work out what you want, and what they want"

THE INEFFECTIVE NEGOTIATOR	THE EFFECTIVE NEGOTIATOR
■ lacks preparation	■ prepares
■ does not have clear objectives	■ has a clear view of what they need to achieve
■ fails to understand the other side's point of view	■ is prepared to listen to the people they deal with
■ has unrealistic expectations	■ will be flexible and look for creative solutions to problems
■ tries to close the deal too quickly	■ will have thought through what is reasonable
■ lacks clarity as to what the deal involves on either side	■ will examine and understand the detail of the agreement
■ gets hung up on areas of disagreement	■ moves from contentious areas to those where agreement can be reached
■ tries to avoid discussing areas that might prove contentious	■ ensures that all problems are eventually dealt with and resolved

Traditional negotiation

Have you ever
thought:

"I won't give in so
easily next time"

"No-one will get away
with that again"

"Just wait until
you need something
from me!"

These are the kinds of
thoughts that the
traditional negotiating
process can produce.

Only a couple of decades ago, the standard view of negotiations was that there were two sides with seemingly opposing objectives. The "game" was to gain as much as possible while giving as little as possible. One side bid high (usually higher than they actually expected to achieve) and the other side bid low (usually lower than they expected to settle for). Each side resisted making concessions and the one that lost least was seen as the winner.

A form of warfare

In this style of negotiation, there is little or no acknowledgment of joint interests. The other side is regarded as the enemy, the negotiation is the battle and the belief that "all's fair in love and war" justifies all behaviour, no matter how childish or unreasonable. Money becomes the only issue and concessions are never given willingly.

A short-sighted approach

Such an approach takes a very short-term view of the relationship between the negotiating parties, and means that the next time you have to deal with the other party the discussion will be coloured on both sides by a desire to settle scores from last time. If you "lost" last time, you will be motivated to try even harder next time to outdo the people you are dealing with.

PLAYING THE GAME

The classic example of old-style negotiation was to be found in wage discussions between employers and unions – two groups with historically conflicting interests and a tendency to treat every negotiation as a power struggle. A typical negotiation would proceed as follows:

1 Union asks for percentage rise in wages (e.g. 8 percent).

2 Employer responds with a low offer (2 percent).

3 Discussions follow, but these take place more as a ritual that must be gone through before agreement is reached than in any real hope of a mutually beneficial outcome.

4 Both sides finally settle for 4 percent – a figure that they were probably prepared to accept all along.

DISADVANTAGES OF THE SHORT-TERM VIEW

An everyday example

- You go to a garage to buy a second-hand car. The salesperson persuades you to pay a certain price (they know that it is more than the car is really worth – they have been less than honest about the history of the car).

- When you buy the car you think you have got a good deal, but over the first few months you discover faults with the car that cost you a great deal of money to rectify.

- You feel cheated by the garage and not only do you decide never to do business with them again but you also take every opportunity to tell family and friends about how badly you were treated.

- The garage appears to have gained on the deal in the short term, but stands to lose in terms of future business and damage to their reputation.

A business example

- A supplier agrees to provide goods or services at a very low price in order to secure an order. Over time he finds that he cannot meet the desired quality standards and still make a profit, so the standards start to slip.

- The customer, who was originally happy with the fact that they had secured supplies at a very low price, becomes dissatisfied when the supplier fails to meet his needs. The relationship becomes increasingly acrimonious.

- The customer will now have to spend time looking for another supplier, and will damage the prospect of future business for the supplier by telling other potential customers about his dissatisfaction. Both parties therefore lose in the long term for what seemed like a short-term gain.

Modern negotiation

Today, thankfully, a much healthier approach is emerging to the whole process of negotiation. There seems to be a recognition that the old regime meant that everyone eventually suffered and that the resulting bad feelings made subsequent business harder to conduct.

An emphasis on partnership

Today's business environment is much more geared towards working together for mutual benefit. You will hear terms such as "partnership" and "strategic alliance" being used to describe the relationships between customers and their suppliers.

EXERCISE

Think of companies or people that you regularly do business with (both in your personal and your business life).

■ Why do you continue to deal with them?

■ What do they do that makes you feel comfortable with the relationship?

■ How do they demonstrate that they understand your needs?

■ How do they resolve problems?

■ What would make you look for an alternative business partner?

Building relationships

The current emphasis on quality issues means that cost can no longer be the sole criterion for a deal. You must also consider the need to build relationships that can continue for a long time – with both parties feeling satisfied, where problems can be sorted out amicably and where future negotiations can be conducted in an atmosphere of mutual interest and support.

Counting the long-term cost

Modern businesses are prepared to take a much longer-term view and to apply a cost/benefit analysis to the outcome of any agreement. What may initially appear to be a low-cost deal can turn out to be expensive in the longer term if both parties do not have a vested interest in maintaining the relationship.

The importance of strategic alliances

Any successful business must recognize that true profit is built through repeat business – long-term beneficial relationships between the customer and supplier. Constantly searching for new customers (or suppliers) is both time-consuming and costly.

Any negotiation should therefore start with both parties recognizing the potential benefits to their respective businesses of establishing a working partnership.

Partnerships and strategic alliances are based on joint interests, and both parties should stand to gain some advantage from reaching agreement and following through with the commitments made. This means that benefits accrued from the relationship can be shared.

OLD STYLE	NEW STYLE
Negotiating from positions	Negotiating about principles
Confrontational	Compromising and collaborating
Self interest	Mutual interests
Short term	Long term
Immediate gains	Ongoing rewards
Getting what I want	Thinking about how the other person feels
The end justifies the means	Bad behaviour may damage this relationship
Thinking the worst of others	Expecting the best of others

What is your negotiating style?

The following exercise is designed to help you think about your own negotiating style and how it could be improved. Read the statements and tick those that you generally agree with. Work through the statements quickly – don't spend too long thinking about them and don't try to work out what the "correct" answer is or to be consistent.

	Statement	Score
1	I like to have look at the issues carefully before I start negotiating.	
2	I often give in on issues for the sake of preserving the relationship.	
3	I am good at consulting others to find out what they really want.	
4	I avoid conflict at all costs.	
5	I sometimes avoid raising issues that I know will create controversy.	
6	I am often the one who proposes the middle ground.	
7	I try never to upset the other person's feelings.	

	Statement	Score
8	I try to think of ways of convincing the other person of the benefits of my position.	
9	I like to get the most contentious issues out in the open as soon as possible.	
10	I am always concerned that both sides are happy with the agreement.	
11	I feel that if you work on the major issues the minor ones will take care of themselves.	
12	I like to negotiate in a friendly or non-confrontational manner.	

	Statement	Score
13	I dislike dealing with people who are aggressive in their manner.	
14	I sometimes feel that I don't express my real concerns.	
15	I feel that if I am always honest it encourages the other person to be the same.	
16	I make sure I always understand the other person's concerns.	
17	I feel that if I give in on some issues this time, it will make the next negotiation easier.	
18	My prime concern is not whether the other person likes me but rather that I get the best deal possible.	
19	I always make sure that when I concede on an issue, I get something back in return.	

	Statement	Score
20	People don't value what they get for nothing.	
21	I like to have plenty of time to think through the implications of any decisions.	
22	If you give people too much time to think about things they are likely to change their mind.	
23	I like to get to know people before we start negotiating.	
24	You have to be careful to separate friendship from business.	

HOW TO SCORE
On the table below, put a tick against the number of those statements that you agreed with. Now count up the number of A, B, C and D answers. The assessments are on pages 20–21.

1 _	B	7 _	D	13 _	C	19 _	A
2 _	D	8 _	B	14 _	C	20 _	A
3 _	B	9 _	A	15 _	B	21 _	B
4 _	C	10 _	D	16 _	D	22 _	A
5 _	C	11 _	A	17 _	D	23 _	D
6 _	D	12 _	C	18 _	A	24 _	B

Totals: A ....   B ....   C ....   D ....

What is your negotiating style?

Remember, you don't have to participate in formal negotiations to work on your skills. Everyday encounters with colleagues will provide plenty of opportunities.

Mostly A

You can be a very tough negotiator, and are probably proud of the fact. You know what you want and are prepared to do whatever you need to get it. You are very good at closing deals but may attempt to push the other person into closing, or fail to take their needs or feelings into consideration. You may end up with "I win: you lose" outcomes, which can create problems if the relationship needs to be ongoing.

Areas to work on

- When preparing for the negotiation, pay more attention to uncovering the other party's expectations and needs.
- In the initial phase, ask more open questions (that is, questions that cannot simply be answered with a "yes" or "no").
- Practice reading other people's body language so that you are more aware of their unspoken feelings and attitudes.
- Spend more discussion time investigating what the other person needs from the agreement.

Mostly B

You probably prepare well for negotiations. You know what is important but you take care to find out the other person's position and are prepared to be flexible to reach agreement on both sides. However, people may find you somewhat formal and clinical in your dealings. They may be intimidated by your style and so hesitate to express their concerns.

Areas to work on

- Try to spend a little more time during the initial discussion developing a personal rapport with the other party.
- Be aware of your own body language, and make sure that it accurately reflects your flexible and open-minded approach to the negotiation.
- If you think the other side is not saying what is on their mind, ask.
- Relax! Let the other side know that you are satisfied with the way the negotiation is progressing.

Mostly C

You probably give away too much in negotiations in an effort to avoid conflict, and may have a tendency to use tentative or unassertive language. You may get "you win: I lose" outcomes more often than you would like.

Areas to work on

- In the preparation phase, decide what it is that you must have from the deal and ensure that those needs are met.
- Think through what you are asking for and why it is important to you so that you can communicate this clearly to others.
- Always prepare a structured agenda – this will help you to ensure that you cover all the issues.
- Work on your body language so that it agrees with your verbal message. Otherwise you may come across as tentative and uncertain.
- Try to see conflict as productive – both sides have to express their conflicting demands before agreement can be reached.

Mostly D

People probably enjoy doing business with you – you strive to deal with people in a friendly and relaxed manner. There is a danger, however, that you will give too much away for the sake of the relationship and fail to focus on those areas which are important to you.

Areas to work on

- Structure your negotiations so that all of the points are dealt with in detail, and you're not tempted to let something go.
- Be honest about your concerns. Remember, the point of establishing a good relationship with the other party is that it should be beneficial to both sides.
- Do not be afraid to express disagreement. Differentiate between saying "No" to the request and "No'" to the person.

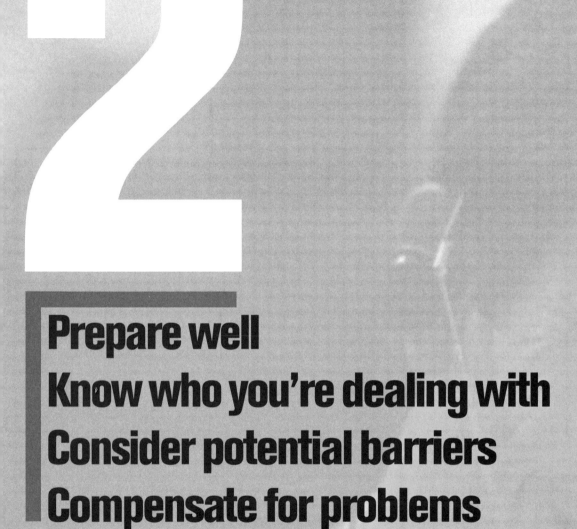

2

Prepare well
Know who you're dealing with
Consider potential barriers
Compensate for problems

What are my limitations?
Whose language is being used?
How much time have we got?

History

Ask yourself the following questions:

■ Has my company dealt with this person before?

■ Have I been briefed on what to expect?

■ If not, where can I get more information?

■ Is there any history of unsatisfactory agreements?

■ What does this person know about me?

■ What are they expecting?

■ Am I different from the person they have dealt with before?

■ Could this be an advantage?

You already know that you never get a second chance to make a first impression. When you are meeting people for the first time you will usually make the effort to get off to the best possible start. However, in negotiations, it is more than possible that there is already some kind of history – either a colleague has already dealt with the other person and passes their opinions on to you, or you have dealt with someone else from the company and they will brief them prior to your first meeting.

Second-hand information

Imagine that your colleague tells you that the person you are about to negotiate with can be very difficult and stubborn and that they drive a hard bargain – mentally you will already be donning a "flak jacket" and expecting the worse. This mind-set can mean you are already erecting barriers between you and them.

It can be very difficult to ignore what others have told you but you can decide to try and set it aside and make up your own mind based on your direct experience of dealing with the person – remember, just because your colleague didn't get on with them doesn't mean that you won't.

Acknowledge former difficulties

If you know there has been a history of poor relationships, you could acknowledge this at the outset of the discussion but make it clear that you want to start off on a different footing and that you are sure that you can conduct business in a friendly manner.

Limitations

Whatever the situation, the parties to a negotiation rarely have complete freedom to lay down terms or agree to conditions. For example, both you and the other person may be working within certain limits as regards budgets or time; you may need to consult someone else for approval of certain aspects of the agreement; or you may not have the necessary knowledge to appreciate the implications of all the variables. Such limitations need not be a hindrance, provided both sides are prepared to be open about them. If, however, this is not the case but you feel that there is a problem, do not be afraid to ask a direct question or admit that you will have to consult with someone who is not currently involved.

THINKING ABOUT LIMITATIONS

Any of the following may apply to you or to the person you are dealing with:

■ Lacks the authority to make the final decision – may need to get final approval from someone more senior.

■ Unclear about the limits within which a deal may be agreed.

■ Unable to be flexible about some of the criteria for agreement (such as quality, quantity, delivery dates etc.) as these have been set by people who will not be present in the negotiation.

■ Does not have the necessary expertise to answer technical questions.

■ Trying to "score points" by being seen to drive a hard bargain.

■ Working against tight deadlines.

■ Lacks knowledge or experience to understand the implications of some aspects of the deal they are asking for.

Language

When you are dealing with someone for whom English is not a first language, you take particular care to ensure that you understand each other. Problems can occur, however, when you think that you are speaking the same language. You can be misled into thinking that both parties share understanding and you will probably not take as much care to check what is meant. How many times have you experienced problems due to misunderstandings that were not identified during the course of a conversation?

The only stupid question is the one you don't ask!

Jargon

All organizations have their own jargon – language that is only used by a specific group of people. Legal and computer specialists are well known for using jargon, but anyone working in a specialized area can fall into the trap.

Jargon can be useful where you are sure that the other person also speaks your language, but it can create problems where each side thinks they know what the other means but fails to check it out.

Ways to ensure understanding

- Never take for granted that both sides hold the same assumptions – always check out that your understanding is shared.
- Avoid abbreviations or shorthand versions – make all explanations explicit, especially when you are dealing with someone who has a specific technical expertise.
- Don't let ego get in the way. Some people feel that asking a question is an admission of stupidity, but if you pretend that you are fully conversant when you are not, you may run into problems further down the line.
- Invite other people to seek clarification of anything you say that is not perfectly clear.
- Remember "Less is more". The best communicators tend to use the simplest, clearest language.

EXERCISE

Can you think of any examples of jargon, abbreviations or technical terminology that are used in your organization?

What could you do to clarify these examples when you are communicating with people outside your organization?

Vague language

Another problematic area is where one or both sides use language which is vague or inexact. This may be just carelessness, or it may reflect an unwillingness to commit to definite action or terms. Tentative wording may also be used to disguise the fact that the speaker doesn't really have the authority to promise a certain concession, but doesn't want to say "no".

Vague language has no place in negotiations. It invariably leads to misunderstanding about what is being asked for, or has been agreed. When you encounter it in discussions, politely ask the speaker to be more exact about what is meant.

The chart below shows some examples of this kind of language, and why it is a problem. As you deal with people, listen for more examples and think about how they could express themselves more clearly. Finally, ask yourself whether you are guilty of using vague language in negotiations.

"Don't assume, ask"

WHAT IS SAID	WHAT'S WRONG WITH IT
A.S.A.P.	This usually means now but is not heard as such. Set a definite deadline.
When you've got time.	This will become a low-priority task which will never get done. Set a definite deadline.
By the end of the week.	This can mean different times to different people. Set a definite deadline.
I think that would be OK.	Sounds unsure. Be more definite.
I'll get back to you on that.	When?
This is fairly important.	It's either important or it isn't. If it is, say so.

Time

One of the most common problems in negotiations is that the parties fail to allow enough time. You need time for discussion, for all necessary information to be provided, for both sides to consider and reflect, and for approval to be obtained from all the relevant people.

Deadlines

In reality, you rarely have as much time as you would like. When you are up against tight deadlines, there is a danger that you will agree to things that you wouldn't have accepted if you had thought about them in more detail. If you feel pressurized, ask yourself whether you would be agreeing to this point if there was more time to discuss it. If the answer is no, you need to consider whether the deadline is more important than the potential problems caused by not getting the details right.

Call for time out

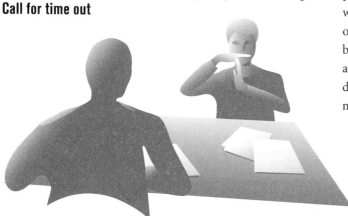

Asking for time

It can never hurt to ask for some time out to consider a deal before agreeing to it. Away from the negotiation table, questions may occur to you that you missed at the time. Sometimes, on reflection, a deal that didn't look too good on Tuesday will seem like a very good deal by Thursday.

Give the other side time

You should also be prepared to give the other person time out to consider their position. Your willingness to do this will give the impression that you have confidence in the quality of the deal. If you put them under pressure to close, they will probably feel that there must be a problem that they haven't seen yet.

Keep things moving

It is important not to lose momentum, particularly if you have put a lot of work into selling your proposals to the other side. If either side asks for time before committing, make sure that you agree to a deadline or a date to renew discussions. You don't want the negotiation to drag on for too long.

Personal conflicts

Personal feelings about the people you are dealing with or the way they do business should not get in the way of your business goals when you are negotiating. In reality, however, they often do. You may find yourself dealing with someone who you don't like, whose manner is puzzling or just plain offensive, or whose approach to the deal you simply can't understand.

Identifying the source of conflict

Often such difficulties arise from basic conflicts in the way the two parties are approaching the negotiation. The first step in this situation is to identify the basis of the conflict. You can then take steps to deal with it. There are three main types of conflict: goal-based, normative-based and judgment-based. The chart below outlines the three types and how to deal with them.

TYPES OF CONFLICT	WHAT IS WRONG	HOW TO DEAL WITH IT
GOAL-BASED (THE "WHAT")	There is little or no agreement as to the eventual outcome or objectives of the negotiation.	Backtrack and discuss both side's objectives, and make sure that mutual benefits have been clearly identified.
NORMATIVE-BASED CONFLICT (THE "HOW")	The goal is shared but both parties have very different views of how it should be reached. One side may have very strong feelings about how things should go.	Spend some time at the beginning of the negotiation to agree the procedural points of the discussion.
JUDGMENT-BASED CONFLICT (FEELINGS)	One side is uncomfortable because they feel, rightly or wrongly, that their feelings or values are not being taken into account.	The best solution is to ask the other person whether they are unhappy with the discussion (see page 26).

Personal conflicts

Recognizing judgment-based conflicts

This is perhaps the hardest area of conflict to deal with because it can be difficult to identify. Typically it is communicated via nonverbal signals – the other person may simply look uncomfortable with what is being said.

If communicated verbally, it may be in the form of what is called "incongruent communication" – that is, there is a perceived mismatch between the words used and the tone of voice or the accompanying body language that leads you to believe that the other person is not entirely behind what they are saying. For example, they might say "Yes, that sounds fine" in a neutral or even doubtful tone.

Uncovering the conflict

If you suspect that a judgment-based conflict is impeding your discussions,

the only thing you can do is to "call" it by saying something like "I get the impression that you are not entirely happy with that point" or "I feel that you may have some concerns about this aspect of the deal". Once the person has expressed their reservations openly, you are in a position to try to deal with them.

If the other party does not acknowledge that there is a problem, there is little more you can do. It may be that you have picked up the wrong message anyway – perhaps they are just tired or thinking about something else entirely.

If you can't uncover the reason for the conflict, it might help to take a break. If either side is letting emotion get in the way of reasonable discussion, this will allow them to calm down and get things in perspective again.

DIFFICULT PEOPLE

We would all prefer to work with people we like and who are like us, but unfortunately this is not possible. On occasion you will have to deal with people that you just don't get on with. If you find that this is the case, ask yourself the following questions.

■ What are they are doing or saying that you find difficult to deal with?

■ Is it relevant or important?

■ Can you choose to accommodate it or simply ignore it?

■ Have you done something that is making them respond negatively to you?

(For more advice on dealing with difficult people and situations, see pages 90–91.)

Helps

Any potential hindrance can be turned upside-down and transformed into a help. By anticipating possible problems and preparing for them, you will help yourself achieve the best possible outcome. The following checklist is designed to help you consider all the possible hindrances.

History

- If there is an existing relationship with your company, set aside any preconceptions about the other person and decide to make your own mind up based on your experience of them.
- If you are meeting the person for the first time, work at making the best possible first impression. Be friendly and make it clear that you want to work with them.

Limits

- Get a clear briefing as to what your authority levels are and what criteria the deal has to meet to be successful.
- Ask the other person if they can actually agree to the deal.

Language

- Check your own language for any company jargon. Aim to communicate simply and clearly.
- Never hesitate to ask the other person to explain any terms that you don't understand.

Time

- Allow enough time for the process, remembering to build in time for reflection on the implications of the proposed deal.
- Offer the other person thinking time – it shows you have confidence in the deal.

Conflicts

- If there is conflict, ask yourself what the basis for the disagreement might be.
- Try to see things from the other person's point of view in order to reduce conflict.
- Be gracious at the end. If you have spent time building up a rapport with the other person and creating common understanding, you want to be able to maximize this in any future negotiations.

A positive attitude is one of the best helps you can have. Decide in advance that you want a successful outcome to the negotiation.

What makes a good agreement?

For a successful agreement, you need to consider all of the following questions. Neglecting to do so may mean that the final deal will cost you more in the long term than you had expected.

Win now, win later

Remember that you have to strike a balance between getting a good deal on this occasion and building a good long-term relationship with the other party. The objective is to settle any differences

1 WILL THE OUTCOME SATISFY MUTUAL INTERESTS?	**2 WILL IT WORK?**	**3 DO BOTH SIDES UNDERSTAND FULLY WHAT HAS BEEN AGREED?**
■ Do both sides feel that they have been dealt with in a fair and equitable manner ? ■ Do both sides feel satisfied, even taking into account compromises that they have had to make?	■ Does it address the needs of both sides? ■ Have all the practical issues been dealt with? ■ Have you considered how you will work together?	■ Have the specifics been discussed and agreed? ■ Has a detailed written agreement been drawn up covering all the required aspects?

within the context of a friendly, ongoing relationship. While trying to resolve any conflict of interests between you and the other party, you need also to focus on those interests that you have in common.

The feelgood factor

A good agreement is not just one that looks good on paper; it is one that both parties feel good about. During discussions, make sure that the other side feels they are being fairly treated.

4 ARE THERE MEASURABLE BENEFITS TO BOTH PARTIES IN TERMS OF SERVICE OR PAYMENT?	5 HAS THE REAL COST OF THE AGREEMENT BEEN CALCULATED?	6 IS THERE AN AGREED REVIEW PROCESS?
■ Does the deal have deliverables with specific deadlines – quantities, qualities, delivery dates, payment schedules and so on? ■ Have expectations been made explicit? ■ Have service level standards been established? ■ Have penalties been agreed for the breaking of service level standards?	■ Do you know exactly what is included in the price? ■ Are there any hidden costs? ■ Does this deal affect any other agreements already in place? ■ Will you need to invest in specialized equipment, facilities or expertise to comply with the agreement? ■ Who will bear the cost of changes to the specifications or increases in the cost of providing the goods or services?	■ How will you know that the agreement is working? ■ Is there a specified time for review on both sides to allow minor problems to be dealt with before they become major ones? ■ How will complaints from either side be dealt with?

3

Preserve good relationships
Prepare a brief
Shop around
Look at the real cost

How much do we have in common?
Whose territory are we on?
Do I need to change my style?

Internal negotiations

Remember that you
and your colleagues
are on the same side.
Don't let internal
competition or bad
feeling prevent you
from focusing on
the main issues of
making the business
more effective.

Negotiations with colleagues and line managers or between departments or divisions can be the most difficult kind. The fact that you know so much about the person you are dealing with can be a hindrance rather than a help, because it is difficult to set aside the history of the relationship and concentrate on the real issues.

Don't get personal

You will need to take particular care not to let your personal situation get in the way of the business to be done. Whether you like or dislike the other person can influence your perceptions of fairness and justice, and how hard you push on issues might be influenced by the fact that you will almost certainly need to have dealings with the other person in the future – you may even have to see them on a daily basis.

Don't assume

There is also a danger that, since you know the other person, you can take too much for granted and assume common understanding of issues and concerns without fully investigating what might lie behind a particular request or decision. It is vital that you look beyond the immediate situation and consider the wider implications of any agreement.

Guidelines for dealing with colleagues

■ Don't let your colleagues feel you are taking them for granted – give them the same respect that you would show to anyone outside your organization.

■ Put your key requests in writing before you hold a meeting. If you give them time to consider your needs, they will probably be more cooperative, and will have time to think about their own interests, too.

■ Try to avoid asking for yes/no decisions immediately – most people respond badly when put under pressure.

■ Consider what you might be able to do for them in return – if you can't think of anything, ask if there is anything that they want or need to make their work easier.

■ Make the effort to deal with colleagues face to face – it can be too easy to pick up the phone or send an e-mail. Most people still prefer the personal touch.

■ If it's you that wants something from them, make the effort to see them on their "home patch".

THE RIGHT APPROACH

It's the busiest time of year at work, but you desperately need a holiday and this is the only month that both you and your partner can get away. When approaching your manager to ask for the time off:

- **Ask face to face:** See them in their office and make sure it's a convenient time for them to talk.
- **Acknowledge their needs:** Explain that you realize it's a bad time to go and that you would have chosen a better time if you could.
- **Provide solutions:** Do your homework in advance, so you can say what key tasks will need to be carried out in your absence and who could do them. This will show your manager that you have considered their side of the situation and are willing to meet them halfway.
- **Offer a trade-off:** Point out that you will be available for overtime for several weeks after your return.

You have a good relationship with the marketing manager, but you've noticed several recurring problems in dealing with their department, and have spent a lot of time coming up with ideas for procedures that would prevent these. When presenting your ideas:

- **Don't presume:** You may get on well with your colleague, but you will still have to tread carefully or they may feel that they are under attack.
- **Do it by the book:** You are dealing with important procedures, so request a meeting in writing and outline the reason, just as you would if dealing with someone you didn't know well.
- **Include all relevant people:** Don't just approach the person you feel most comfortable with. Think about who will be affected and discuss your ideas with everyone involved.
- **Let them express their needs:** Make it clear that, although you have initiated the process of change, you are open to their suggestions for improvements. Be prepared to have more than one meeting so that a dialogue can take place.

Negotiations with customers

One way to keep customers, following the lead set by many retailers recently, would be to establish a loyalty scheme. Is there any way, other than by lowering your prices, that you could recognize long-standing or regular customers?

Whether you are trying to win over new customers or retain existing ones, negotiating with them can be tricky. The customer is usually in a position of power during the negotiation, because you want their business. You need to balance meeting their needs with the benefits of the deal to you.

Winning new customers

Negotiations with a potential new customer provide you with an opportunity to show them that you can meet their needs and that you will be easy to do business with.

During the negotiation, you should aim to demonstrate that:

- you understand their situation
- you want to help them achieve their objectives
- time spent with you will be pleasant and productive, and will not add to their troubles
- they can share their concerns and problems with you in an open way
- you are bringing "added value" to the deal – perhaps by offering them something that other similar suppliers will not
- any problems that arise will be dealt with swiftly and effectively.

Following up

Once a deal is done, it is a good idea to call your customer from time to time to check that everything is going smoothly. This will avoid the customer forming the impression that you have put more effort into securing his business than into fulfilling the agreement.

Looking after existing customers

With customers who have been with you for some time, you still need to stress how much you value their business and the relationship you have with them. It is easy to take a long-standing customer for granted, and to assume that they will always continue to place their business with you. Never forget that they have a choice.

However, there are several points in your favour if you have been with a customer for a long time, and it is important that your customer should recognize these intangible benefits in any ongoing negotiations.

- Both parties have an investment in the relationship.
- You understand each other's business.
- Changing suppliers would cost your customer time and money.

Keeping your customers

At some point in any business relationship, all customers wonder if they could get their supply from another source, perhaps at a lower cost. They may even tell you that they plan to talk to alternative suppliers. What the customer is saying, in effect, is that they wish to review your agreement with a view to renegotiating certain aspects of it.

What not to do

The temptation at this point is to offer the customer a discount in order to keep their business (sometimes referred to as "low-balling"). This is the wrong thing to do for two reasons.

■ The first and obvious reason is that you will be making less money on the deal.

■ The second is that your customer may interpret this as proof that you have been charging them too much in the past.

What to do

Arrange a meeting with your customer to talk about any concerns they have with the current arrangement. Usually when a customer starts to complain about the price there is an underlying issue which has started them thinking about it, and a discussion will give you the opportunity to find out what this is.

■ Reassure the customer that your costs are indeed reasonable for the quality of the product or service you provide.

■ If they are quoting lower prices from alternative suppliers, make sure that they are comparing like with like. A deal that looks similar on the surface may have hidden costs that they have not fully considered.

■ Stress the value of the fact that you understand the way they work and that the cost of having to establish that level of understanding with someone new.

■ Consider offering a discount but only in exchange for some alteration in the arrangement – bulk or regular orders, adjustments to specification or shorter payment terms, for example.

All customers want to feel that they are the most important people that you deal with. Making customers feel special is a key factor in building a relationship and ensuring that it continues.

Negotiations with suppliers

As a customer, you may find yourself in the situation of negotiating with several suppliers at once as you look around for the best deal.

You should be looking not only for a supplier who can meet your requirements, but one with whom you will feel comfortable. If you don't like and get on with them during the negotiation, you are unlikely to enjoy doing business with them in the future. It is up to the supplier to convince you that they are willing to help you meet your needs.

Preparing a brief

When you are looking for a new supplier it can be very helpful to both sides if you draw up an initial briefing document that outlines your requirements. There are several advantages to providing prospective suppliers with such a brief.

- Suppliers who are unable or unwilling to meet your requirements will exclude themselves.
- Those suppliers who pitch for your business will be well prepared, will have thought about the questions you might have and should have prepared suitable documentation to help you make your decision. All of this will save you time.
- By having prospective suppliers answer your brief point by point, you will be in a position to compare like with like when looking at their proposals, instead of finding that none of them has supplied the information you need.

AREAS TO BE COVERED BY A BRIEF MIGHT INCLUDE:

- **expected budget**
- **quality standards**
- **quantities required**
- **order lead times**
- **delivery dates**
- **stockholding arrangements**
- **invoicing and payment arrangements**
- **contract review dates**
- **how problems will be resolved**

Existing suppliers: getting a better deal

Just as a supplier can start to take his customers for granted, there is a danger that, as a customer, you can become too comfortable with a particular supplier and so fail to regularly review and update the arrangement.

Even if there are no obvious problems, it is still necessary to assess the contract from time to time. With long-standing suppliers you need to hold regular review meetings to ensure that both sides are up to date with requirements and to identify any potential problem areas.

You probably already do this in your private life. If you have savings, for example, you probably check from time to time to see whether you are getting the best interest rate available. Often this does not involve changing financial institution, but rather shifting your money from one kind of savings account to another.

The same can apply to dealings with your suppliers at work. By regularly reviewing your business agreement, you can request changes in their terms or their procedures that will deliver benefits for you.

COUNTING THE COST

If you have concerns or problems with a current supplier it may be easier and more cost-effective to discuss the issues with them and give them an opportunity to deal with the problems than to go out into the open market again.

If your main concern is getting the cheapest deal possible, you may end up with a supplier who fails to meet the detailed aspects of your requirements. Make sure that any prospective new supplier offering a good price can still meet all your specifications, including quality.

The process of finding a new supplier, putting a deal in place and getting the new arrangements up and running can be costly in terms of both time and money. If you are constantly switching from one supplier to another on the basis of price alone, you may be incurring hidden costs that outweigh any saving on price.

4

Structure your approach
Know your goals
Choose your time
Set boundaries

Can I do this alone or do I need help?
What must I get from this deal?
What can I give away?

Preparation

All negotiations have a life cycle – a series of stages that need to be gone through to ensure that the criteria for a good agreement are met. Applying a structure to the negotiation process can help you ensure that you avoid potential dangers and that you have addressed all your requirements – and those of the other party – in detail. Before entering into any negotiation, you need to consider the five questions given below.

1 What is your objective?
■ What should a good agreement include?
■ What can you not do without?
■ What are your expectations of the other party in the negotiation?

2 What are your limits?
■ What level of authority do you have?
■ Will you need to get final clearance prior to final agreement?
■ What is non-negotiable ?

3 Who are you negotiating with?
■ What do you know about them already?
■ What can you find out about them?
■ What might their requirements be?
■ Will they bring any non-negotiable areas to the discussion?

4 Are you dealing with the person who can "sign off" the deal?
■ Will they have the authority to sign the contract?
■ Will they have any limits on what they can agree to?
■ Will they need to get clearance from someone else before they can sign an agreement?
■ If so, how can you help them to recommend the deal?

5 What would be unacceptable?
■ At what point would you walk away from the deal?
■ At what point would any short-term benefits from the deal be outweighed by the long-term costs?

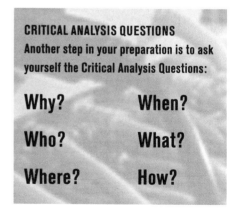

CRITICAL ANALYSIS QUESTIONS
Another step in your preparation is to ask yourself the Critical Analysis Questions:

Why?   **When?**

Who?   **What?**

Where?   **How?**

Why?

The first of the critical analysis questions, "why?", actually should be broken down into two questions: "Why am I doing this?" and "Why me?"

Why am I doing this ?

You need to be quite clear what your desired outcome is for the negotiation. If you haven't identified clear objectives for the discussion, then the probability of your needs being met is diminished. You also need to have specific requirements for the deal. For example, you may be meeting with a supplier to secure a lower price for your regular order because you have realized that the market for the particular product has changed and you could get it more cheaply elsewhere. In such a case it would be essential to know how much of a reduction you want and what you would be prepared to accept.

Why me?

The second question to ask yourself is "Why am I the best person to conduct this negotiation?" Think about the skills, experience or knowledge that you will bring to the negotiating table. Does your relationship with the person you will be dealing with make you particularly suitable? For example, have you dealt with them successfully before or will you be responsible for the agreement during its implementation?

When answering this second "why" question, you also need to consider the limits of what you can achieve. Consider whether other people would be able to help. Would it be helpful to have other people there during the negotiation ? Are there other people who it would be useful to consult prior to the final agreement ? Who will need to be informed once the agreement has been reached?

The saying "to fail to prepare is to prepare to fail" is never more true than in negotiating. The only place where agreement comes before preparation is in a dictionary.

NEGOTIATION AS A JOURNEY

It may help to think of the negotiation as a journey. When you go on a journey, you need to know both your starting point (in terms of the negotiation, this would mean information such as history, limitations and so on) and your desired destination (the outcome) in order to plan your route. The specific requirements are the criteria that need to be met for the deal to be viable, and these may be thought of as places you will pass on route, which help to reassure you that you are travelling in the right direction.

Who?

You may be entering into a negotiation with someone you have encountered before, or with someone who has no history with you or your company. Either way, you should take the time to find out something about the person or people you will be dealing with.

Know your history

If there is an established relationship with the other party, do all you can to find out about them and what they are likely to bring to the negotiation. Know who you are dealing with.

- What do you know about them or what can you find out?
- Whom should you ask? Is your source's view likely to be coloured by personal concerns?
- What are the interests, needs and concerns of the person you will be dealing with?
- What is the history of the relationship?

If there have been problems in the past, it may be wise to acknowledge these openly in the beginning, stressing that you have taken steps to avoid similar problems in the future, rather than hope that they don't bring them up. On the other hand, if they have had a good business relationship with one of your colleagues, acknowledge that relationship and stress that your intention is to continue it.

Do some detective work

If the person you are dealing with is a prospective new customer or supplier, it is still worth trying to find out something about them – any information could help to strengthen your position.

- If they are a potential customer, are they approaching you as an alternative to an existing supplier?
- If they are a supplier, who are their existing customers? Does their customer base inspire confidence?
- Have they been given any industry awards or has there been any favourable press coverage about them recently? Most people are flattered by the fact that you have taken the trouble to find out something like this.
- Do you know, or can you find out, anything about them on a personal level? People like to be treated as individuals. It doesn't have to be anything very personal – just knowing what football team they support, for example, could help break the ice.

Where?

Location may not seem like a very important issue but it can be crucial. The fundamental question is: "Your place or mine?"

Your place

The general rule is if you are selling, you should go to the customer – you should be seen to be the one making the most effort.

This is not simply a matter of courtesy. Visiting the customer on their own territory can work in your favour. Surprisingly, people are usually easier to sell to when they are on their home ground. They feel more comfortable and relaxed and are therefore more receptive.

People are also inclined to be more polite when you are a guest in their office or home. This is why many financial service agents prefer to visit you at home.

Many people think, wrongly, that the best thing to do is to invite prospective customers to their location so that they can show them hospitality. This is advisable for the second meeting but rarely for the first one.

My place

When you are being sold to or asked for your cooperation, you should expect the other party to come to you.

Remember, though, that they are guests on your territory and treat them accordingly. Whether you decide to do business with them or not, the way you deal with them reflects on you and your company. You do not want to develop a reputation for being discourteous or a difficult person to do business with.

Neutral territory

If you feel that there are grounds for conflict, it may be better to meet on neutral ground. High-level diplomatic negotiations, for example, are often held in neutral countries. Internal negotiations may be an exception to the "your place/my place" rule. Booking a meeting room can ensure that neither side feels at a disadvantage.

If you are visiting a prospective client to make a presentation, check that you will be able to use any equipment that you need. Valuable time is often wasted while prospective suppliers struggle to set up their presentation.

THE ROUND TABLE APPROACH

The layout of the location can influence the atmosphere of a negotiation. Diplomatic negotiations usually take place at a round table so that no-one has a prime position. In old-style management v. union negotiations, the two parties would line up on opposite sides of the table. This created an adversarial atmosphere at the outset and probably made agreement harder to reach. If you have a choice, a round table can help to create an feeling of intimacy and rapport. If you are negotiating as part of a team, try to avoid sitting together, as this can create an appearance of defensiveness.

When?

Timing can be crucial. The best time for the negotiation to begin is when everybody has been fully briefed and knows what to expect. Make sure that you, your colleagues and the other party have all been given a brief outline of the issues you will want to cover and let them know when you intend to call or meet them. If you are dealing internationally, do remember to take the time difference into account.

What time?

Even a detail such as the time of day when the meeting takes place can make a difference. Don't be tempted to play the power game of asking for breakfast meetings at impossibly early times, just to give the impression that you are extremely important and busy – this will irritate everyone else.

Schedule meetings for a time when everyone is relaxed and at their best – mid-morning is usually a good time. If the discussions are likely to be complex, don't try to fit them all into one meeting, as people's concentration will start to fail. Allow plenty of time for breaks in an all-day meeting, and remember that people will not be at their most alert after a heavy lunch.

Ready or not?

Do not be pressured into a negotiation before you have had time to prepare. Reschedule if you are not ready. Equally, you should resist the urge to pressure the other side just because you are ready. This is particularly important if you are negotiating over the phone – always check that it is convenient for the other person to deal with the matter at that time. If you interrupt them or catch them unprepared, it can make them less inclined to cooperate.

TIMING CHECKLIST

■ Allow adequate preparation time

■ Will everyone be available?

■ Allow an adequate length of time for the meeting

■ Time of day

■ Make sure the general conditions will be good for you. For example, make sure that the meeting will not come immediately before an important deadline has to be met at work.

What?

The next question in your critical analysis is simple: what do you want to achieve? The answer to this may be simple – "I want a stereo system with reasonable sound for less than £200" – or it may be more complex, involving issues of cost, quality, variety, delivery and more.

What do I need?

If your negotiation is of the more complex kind, make a checklist of what you need from the agreement. For example, suppose a shoe retailer is looking for a supplier of women's fashion shoes. Concerns might include:

- price
- profit margin
- quality
- wide range of styles
- wide range of sizes
- ability to fulfil orders at short notice
- discounts for large orders
- guaranteed delivery dates
- guaranteed stock availability

What is most important to me?

The next step is to prioritize your checklist into what you must have, what would be useful to have and what would simply be nice to have.

These will depend on the situation. In the case of the shoe retailer, a "nice-to-have" term might be the ability to fulfil orders at short notice. However, if they were buying sandals, and sales varied from one week to the next according to the weather, then that term might be more important, even becoming a "must-have".

What am I prepared to give?

An additional area to think about is what you are prepared to concede in order to do the deal. You might decide that discounts are not a crucial factor, and that you would be able to forego them in return for something – perhaps a guarantee that prices would not rise before a certain date, or an earlier delivery date.

KILLER CONCERNS

When making your checklist, ask yourself whether there are any "killer concerns" – conditions that would kill the deal if they could not be met. For example, a large retail chain might insist that the style of any shoe they bought must be exclusive to them. If you have such a concern, you should make it clear to the other party as early as possible in the discussions that this point is not negotiable.

How?

The last of your critical analysis questions is "How?" There are so many means of communication now that you have more choice than ever before. You can negotiate:
■ face to face
■ over the phone
■ in writing – by letter, fax or e-mail.

Face to face

Meeting face to face can provide you with vital evidence as to how the person you are dealing with feels about the situation. This evidence – provided by tone of voice, facial expression and body language – is missing in any other form of communication.

Over the phone

Because nonverbal signals are missing when you talk to someone on the telephone, it may be best to reserve this method for negotiating with people you know well. It is usually helpful, however, to supplement face-to-face discussions with telephone calls just to confirm details or check progress.

In writing

Face-to-face dialogue may be best, but written communication still plays a vital part in negotiations. Written briefs, summaries of proposed agreements and minutes of meetings all have their role to play.

A disadvantage of written communication, however, is that your tone can easily be misinterpreted. For example, if the recipient has had a bad day, he may take offence at a message that you believed to be neutral in tone when you wrote it.

WHEN TO MEET
■ for initial discussions, once everybody concerned has been briefed in writing
■ for interim discussions if the negotiation is complex
■ to hammer out the fine details before closing

WHEN TO PHONE
■ to provide a quick answer to any queries the other party may have raised
■ to confirm that action has been taken as promised
■ to chase action or information from the other party

WHEN TO WRITE
■ to brief all parties before the initial discussion
■ to confirm what has been agreed in talks so far
■ to confirm key information (such as price) that has been given over the phone
■ when setting out the final agreement

Non-negotiables

The phrase "everything is negotiable" is not really true. In any deal you need to be clear that there may be certain restrictions. Some things cannot be offered within a negotiation, because negotiating around them at the outset will lead to problems later.

Standards

Such non-negotiables are often known as "standards". Standards are objective criteria which bring independent measures of fairness, efficiency or scientific merit to the process of the negotiation. Ideally they should exist independently of the negotiating parties and be both legitimate and practical. It is vital that you recognize these standards prior to your negotiation and it may be helpful to express them explicitly at the opening stages of the discussion.

Legal requirements

A contract may have to follow a specific format to be legally binding. Sometimes certain licences or permissions need to be obtained prior to agreement. For instance, a firm that prints T-shirts could not undertake to produce shirts with the image of a copyrighted character without obtaining the necessary permissions first from the copyright holder. A contract that required one of the parties involved to break the law would be invalid. For example, it would be illegal for a recruitment agency to take a contract that required them to discriminate against certain groups where the law forbids such discrimination.

Health and safety

Contravention of safety requirements could lead to prosecution or personal liability claims and make any insurance cover invalid. For example, a transport company could not offer delivery schedules that would involve their drivers working longer than the legal maximum shift. To take another example, a toy company could not offer to cut costs by modifying their toys in a way that would stop them complying with safety regulations.

Non-negotiables

VIDEO ARTS

"What's their bottom line?"

Overhead costs

Some overheads, such as the costs of materials or labour (particularly if there are minimum wage regulations) may be unalterable. Time – for example, the staff time required to service a deal – is often forgotten as an overhead cost.

Professional codes of conduct

Many professions and industries have regulatory bodies that lay down codes of conduct. Practices that break these codes could leave an individual or company open to prosecution or disbarment from their profession.

For instance, a hospital might agree to sell information on its use of drugs to a pharmaceutical firm carrying out market research, but it could not provide any patient details, as that would break confidentiality. To take another example, a builder might have to refuse to install a stairs or bathroom in a particular space because it would not comply with building regulations.

Market value and market rate

The perceived value or goods and services is often a matter of opinion and subject to change or the laws of supply and demand. However, in some cases values may be determined by an external body which decides what is fair and reasonable, and widely accepted within an industry. In such cases, it will be non-negotiable.

Ethics

Very few people would be prepared to enter into an agreement that involves what they would consider improper practices. These could include bending the law, breaking confidentiality, undercutting competitors, deception, endangering people's safety or unfair treatment of employees.

DEALING WITH NON-NEGOTIABLE REQUESTS

If the person you are dealing with attempts to put a non-negotiable on the table, make it quite clear that you are unable to meet that request.

Ask, however, why they want it. By uncovering why it is important to them, you may be able to come up with an alternative that will meet their needs without contravening any non-negotiable standards.

The escape hatch

Having considered all of the critical analysis questions, you also need to think about the point at which you might decide that agreement will not be reached. When would the cost/benefit equation not make sense for you? What stipulations in the contract might make delivery very difficult or impossible?

It may seem negative to think about what would kill the deal, but preparing for it and having your "fall back" position ready, can help you to feel and behave more confidently.

Prepare a "parting shot"

If you reach deadlock in a negotiation, your main objective should be to exit with dignity. You should leave the other party with the message that even though doing business is not possible at this time, you would be happy to do business at a later date.

Even if you feel that your time has been wasted, you will need to keep your cool – a display of temper or sulking is unlikely to create the desired effect. If the other party has behaved badly and you feel you never want to do business with them again, you should still treat them with respect. Remember that your behaviour should reflect well on you and on your company.

Prepare a "fall-back" position

As well as deciding what would be unacceptable, you should also think about what you will do if the negotiation breaks down.

If you are the customer, consider whether:

- there are alternative suppliers who could meet your needs
- you could strengthen your position by talking informally to them prior to the negotiation.

If you are the supplier consider whether:

- there are other markets for your goods or services
- you can recoup any investment made in researching or preparing your proposal by using your knowledge to approach potential customers in the same sector.

5

Prepare an agenda
Explore wants and needs
Build agreement
Close the deal

Who is setting the agenda?
What lies behind their demands?
Should I offer concessions?

Setting the agenda

Your preparation, if you have done it thoroughly, will provide you with a comprehensive agenda – a list of areas that need to be covered for you to get the deal you require. You will also have recognized why these things are important to you and so will be able to communicate your needs in a clear, convincing and confident manner.

A shared agenda

Once you have drawn up your own agenda, it is a good idea to set it out in writing and give the other party a copy in advance of the meeting. If you are doing this, you may also wish to indicate what is not on the agenda: issues that you feel are outside the scope of the negotiation.

The point of sending the agenda to the other party is not to take control of the discussions, but to allow them to contribute. Emphasize that the agenda is still a draft at this stage and that they can add items to it. Inviting their input in this way means that you can create a climate of agreement even before the discussions begin.

Creating a structure

While it may seem very formal, an agenda can help to give your discussions a structure. Setting out your concerns will help the other party to think through theirs, if they haven't done so already. Once you have agreed the key areas where agreement need be reached, you are in a better position to set the pace of the discussion.

Making the agenda work for you

When you are preparing your agenda, aim to place items that you think will be easy to agree at the top of the list.

There are two advantages to this. The first is that it gets everybody into the right frame of mind – one of mutual agreement. If you place contentious items at the beginning, you can develop a negative atmosphere in which all points will be contested.

The second advantage is that, as the negotiation progresses, the more areas of agreement that are established, the more willing people will be to compromise on the more contentious points. Because they have already invested time and energy in the discussion, their emotional need to resolve conflict increases.

The last minute

Even if everyone has already seen the agenda, it is a good idea to recap it briefly at the outset of the meeting. This allows for last-minute changes and focuses attention on the coming discussion.

SAMPLE AGENDA

■ Prices and specifications

■ Delivery dates

■ Warehousing arrangements

■ Key personnel

■ Review system

Needs, wants and interests

After opening the discussion in a professional, structured way, you are now ready to enter the next phase – one of exploration.

During this phase, possibilities are identified and discussed, and you need to create an atmosphere where both sides feel free to be open and honest. This, however, may take some effort to achieve. You need to be able to differentiate between three things:

■ needs – those things that people feel they cannot do without
■ wants – those things that people would prefer to have
■ interests – the reasons that may lie behind wants and needs.

The exploration process

■ When someone states a need or a want, ask why.

■ Encourage them to explain why what they are asking for is so important to them.

■ Try to understand the situation from their point of view.

■ Show that you want to help them meet their needs, wants and interests.

■ Be prepared to be honest about your own interests so the other person can meet you halfway.

Why exploration is important

Each time a want or need is identified, you should explore the situation by asking for more information. Needs and wants are what people first talk about. They are taking up a position by identifying what they think the final outcome should include. It can sound like a non-negotiable list.

If you only talk about needs and wants, you may find it very difficult to negotiate because the two sides may seem to have little in common. The important thing to remember at this stage is that wants are often only opening salvos and should be treated in this light. Exploration will help you to understand why the other person is asking for something and to make sense of what might at first appear to be unreasonable demands.

Move to the middle ground

Once you understand what lies behind the other person's demands, you will be able to suggest alternatives that will address their requirements.

By showing the other person that you understand their position, you can reduce their resistance to your alternative suggestions. In addition, they will be more ready to make concessions to you. You are now in a position to move to the middle ground.

CASE STUDY: THE PAY INCREASE

STATING WANTS AND NEEDS

An employee goes to his manager and asks for a pay rise. He says he WANTS an increase of 5 percent, and that he NEEDS it because the cost of living has risen.

The manager's initial response is to refuse. He feels the employee's demand is unreasonable. He says that he WANTS to ensure the smooth running of the department, and to do this he NEEDS to keep tight control over his salary bill.

EXPLORATION

The employee and manager now need to consider the implications of their conversation and explore each other's INTERESTS. Is the employee saying that he will leave if he doesn't get the pay increase? Is the manager saying that there are no circumstances under which an increase could be awarded?

UNCOVERING INTERESTS

It emerges that the employee feels that he is currently not being adequately compensated for the work he is doing because of an increase in responsibilities. He also suspects that some of his colleagues are earning more for comparable work.

The manager is anxious to be seen by his senior management as someone who controls overhead costs effectively. He also fears that if he gives one employee an increase then others will expect the same. He is aware that the company is considering outsourcing work as a method of controlling costs.

MOVING TOWARDS AGREEMENT

The two are now in a position to address each other's interests. The manager reassures the employee that he is being paid the same as his colleagues. However, he acknowledges that the employee has recently taken on additional responsibilities, and adds that he is doing a good job. The employee concedes that he is anxious for an increase partly because he needs more money but also because he wishes his contribution to be recognized. He realizes that if costs are not kept down and the company outsources work, jobs will be at risk, including his own.

THE DEAL

They agree on a 2½ percent pay rise with immediate effect if the employee agrees to take on some additional tasks. He will also have a new job title to reflect his increased responsibility. This satisfies the employee's need for recognition, and also means that other employees cannot expect to receive the same pay rise.

CASE STUDY: THE HOUSE PURCHASE

You have found the house that you want to buy. You WANT to pay £60,000, but the seller WANTS more. You NEED to stay within certain limits, but the buyer NEEDS to get a good price. There seems to be little room for negotiation unless you can explore the situation and uncover interests. The answers to the following questions may help you arrive at a solution:

■ Does the price they are asking for affect their next purchase?
■ Is it in their interest to be able to move quickly?
■ Would the fact that you are not in a hurry to move help them to accept your offer?
■ Can they include anything extra that would make the asking price more acceptable to you?
■ Are they in a "chain" which would be affected by their having to look for a new buyer if you pull out?

By getting a fuller picture, you will be better able to resolve your contradictory positions. Suppose it turns out that the seller needs to make a quick sale because they are moving abroad to take up a new job. The final solution might be that the seller agrees to include carpets, curtains and kitchen appliances – which they don't want to take with them anyway. You agree to pay an extra £3,000, which you can now afford because you had budgeted this amount for the included items, and you also undertake to complete the sale within two months to meet the buyer's deadline for moving.

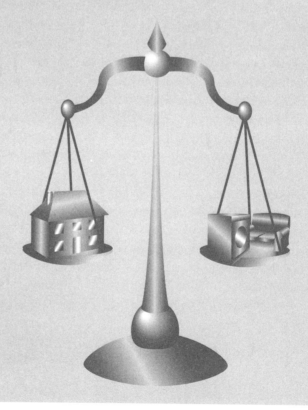

The middle ground

Once you have both uncovered the interests that lie behind your opening positions and have clearly stated what your own interests are, you can move to a stage of bidding and proposing. In order to reach a WIN:WIN outcome, both sides will need to be prepared to compromise.

Moving towards agreement

At this stage it should be clear that you are only exploring possibilities – neither side is required to give a firm commitment.

You are asking the other party to consider what a good deal would need to look like. If you make a proposal and they say they cannot accept it, ask, "Why not?" By getting them to explain what is unacceptable about the proposal, you may be able to think of an alternative that would overcome their objections or concerns. Ask "What if" questions as a way to move forward: "What if we could offer you a shorter delivery time at a slightly higher cost on urgent orders?"

If this approach fails to uncover their reservations, you may need to establish boundaries by asking direct questions: "What would be the minimum order that you could agree to?"

Variables

As you explore the possibilities, it is important to be clear in your mind what the variables in the deal are. These are aspects of the deal that can change. You will have identified most of these in the preparation stages – they could include price and certain aspects of the specification, for instance.

However, you may uncover more variables in the exploratory stage, either because the other side proves to be more flexible than you had expected, or because they introduce a new possibility. For example, in the case study on page 59, the employee began the discussion thinking that the only variable was money. However, in the final deal, improved status and a new job title were part of the package that he accepted.

"Look for variables"

The middle ground

Don't concede – exchange

During the stage of trading and bartering to reach the middle ground, it is wise to ensure that whenever you agree to a concession in the other person's favour, you get something back in return.

It is well known that people tend to place little or no value on things they feel that they got for nothing. This means that if you give things away too easily, the other person may fail to appreciate the true cost of the concession to you. For example, if you easily agree to supply something "a couple of days earlier" the recipient may fail to appreciate that this will mean working until midnight for the week before the new delivery date.

Although you do not want to involve a customer or supplier in your own business too deeply, it is as well to ensure that the other people understand that there is some kind of cost. For example, you may ask for slightly earlier payment in return.

The exchange does not need to be of equal value – what is important is that both sides have shown flexibility in order to keep the discussion in balance.

From your point of view the best concessions are those that have high perceived value to the recipient while having low cost (in real terms) to the donor. For example, in the case study of the house buyer (page 60) the seller needs to move quickly. If the buyer is in a position to do so – perhaps because he has no house of his own to sell – then he can give the buyer something he badly needs at no inconvenience to himself.

KEEP THE DISCUSSION MOVING

If at any point you hit an area where agreement or compromise is proving difficult to achieve, it could be advisable to set it aside and move to another less contentious area on the understanding that you will return to it at a later time. Remember that at this point you are only looking for agreement in principle – neither side is giving absolute commitment.

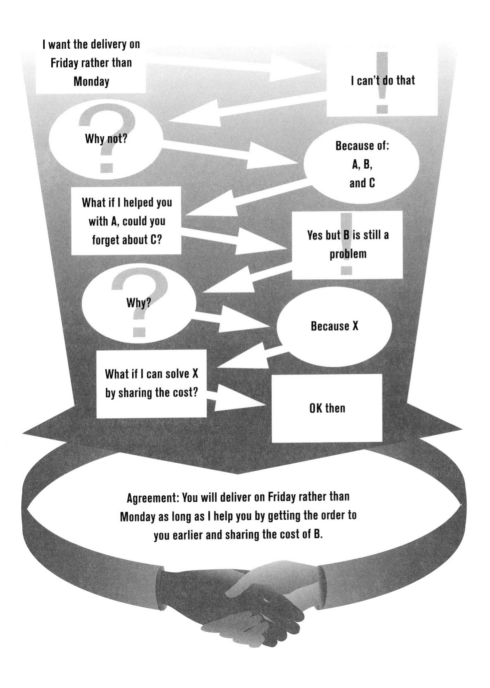

Firming up proposals

You are now in a position to start closing the deal. You have covered all the issues and explored the possibilities, and are broadly in agreement. You will have been taking notes of points agreed throughout the discussion. The close should be a question of confirming the specifics.

Restate your case

On each point it can be helpful to go through a process of restating what the want or need was and to summarize what was finally agreed. For example, "We need delivery on Mondays instead of Tuesdays, as you initially proposed. You have agreed that you can do this if we get our order to you by noon on Friday – is that correct?" Keep checking that the other party is satisfied with the summary. Look for non-verbal signals as well as what is said.

Minimize differences

You can use the restating approach to resolve any outstanding issues: "So,

we've agreed on A, B, and C. That only leaves D to be decided." The intent here is to stress how much progress you have both made in reaching agreement and to minimize the perception of any remaining differences.

Write it down

The act of writing down each point agreed can act as a positive reinforcement of the negotiation process. It shows the other party that the discussion has moved into a new phase, away from exploration and towards resolution. After the discussion, you should type up your handwritten notes and send a copy to the other party as confirmation.

If you are not negotiating face-to-face at this stage, it is even more important to let the other party see the current agreement in writing rather than just going over it on the phone. Seeing the agreement in writing may prompt some final questions that are best dealt with at this stage. Prevention is always better than cure.

The agreement trail

Sometimes you may feel that the deal is all but done and it's time to close, and yet the other party is dithering about seemingly minor details. If this is the case, it may be time to use the agreement trail.

What is the agreement trail?

This is a technique used especially in sales and by those who design opinion polls. It is also sometimes known as the "assumptive close".

The intent is to ask a series of questions that are designed to elicit a specific final response. The questions are either closed or leading in a way that encourages the person to answer positively. In negotiations, this technique is generally employed by the person who is perceived as the "seller".

How does it work?

The theory underlying this approach is that on the whole people strive to be consistent. If you can get them to agree with seemingly small points, they will find it difficult and contradictory to disagree when it comes to the final and most important question. It tests the state of readiness of the "buyer" and gives a final opportunity to identify any remaining concerns.

It is like driving along a road and coming to traffic lights. A "yes" is the equivalent of a green light allowing you to continue along the road. At a "no", or red light, you must stop. In negotiating terms this means you need to stop and deal with the objection. Once the objection is overcome, the light is green again and you can move on.

A POSITIVE RESPONSE
The beauty of using this technique is that if at any stage someone raises an objection it can be dealt with and overcome, ensuring that you can be sure of a positive response to the final question.

THE AGREEMENT TRAIL IN ACTION

"So, we've looked at all of your requirements."
"We've agreed that our company can meet both your quality standards and delivery dates."
"You agree that you can guarantee minimum monthly orders in return for a discount of 5 percent."
"You've said that, based on all of this, you are in a position to sign the deal today."
"So, shall we go ahead and draw up the contract?"

Closing

Always put your agreement in writing. What people regard as an unwritten understanding rarely is.

When the end is in sight, you may be tempted to push for commitment. However, it is important to avoid doing this prematurely. A satisfactory agreement that has been thoroughly explored to the mutual satisfaction of both parties may take more time, but it will usually produce better and more workable outcomes that are more likely to stand the test of time.

Just as you structured the discussion itself, so the final agreement will benefit from having a definite format. The following checklist should help you make sure you've covered everything.

Checklist for closure

- Make a complete list of issues from both sides.
- Prepare a draft framework for agreement – stress that it is only a framework at this stage. The draft should mention areas which still need to be agreed, leaving the details to be completed – for example, "Invoice and payment deadlines to follow".
- Firm up the agreement by tackling any outstanding details. For example, "We will invoice by the 27th of each month and you will ensure payment within 30 days".
- Record each point as it is agreed.

- Ensure that you set down a process for reviewing the agreement. Will you need to meet on a regular basis to improve the deal in the light of operational experience? What would be a suitable review period? Is the agreement designed to cover only a stated period of time?
- Agree a procedure for dealing with complaints or problems that arise. For example, "Any queries regarding invoice amounts are to be addressed directly to the Finance Director. Amendments to payment terms can only be agreed between the Financial Director and the Director of the invoicing company."

WARNINGS

- If at this stage any key point is re-opened for negotiation, then all issues may be re-opened for negotiation. You need to view any changes in terms of the possible implications for the deal as a whole.

- Know when to stop talking once you have established final agreement. Many successful negotiations have been ruined by people who haven't known when to shut up.

Don't get stuck

As you approach your goal, it's all the more important to keep things moving and not get bogged down in details. Remember the strategies that have helped you to get this far.

- If you are still having problems agreeing specific points, move to those where there is consensus. Use the level of agreement to encourage problem resolution. "So, we've agreed on three-quarters of the points – what can we do to agree on what's left?"
- If a "killer concern" (something that could prevent final agreement) is identified, both parties may benefit from taking time out to consider the implications of failure to agree.
- Focus on issues and away from personalities.
- Give recognition for any concessions the other party has made.
- Give the the other party a final opportunity to clarify any issues.

A SMART AGREEMENT
Whatever the final agreement looks like, it should always comply with SMART criteria:

Specific	Everyone in the negotiation should know what has been agreed in detail.
Measurable	There should be tangible, defined benefits on both sides. Make sure that all parties will be able to see and judge progress once the agreement is implemented.
Agreed	Both sides have explicitly expressed their commitment to the agreement. This could mean everyone signing a written agreement or shaking hands.
Realistic	It is a deal that can be implemented. Make sure that you have agreed a practical plan, and that everyone involved is in a position to meet the terms that they have committed to.
Time-bound	The agreement has a stated life cycle with agreed review dates.

6

**Observe
Question
Listen
Respond**

**What interpersonal skills do I need?
What personal impact am I making?
Is it helping or hindering the process?**

Observing

Why do you feel more comfortable dealing with some people than others? Why do you sometimes get the feeling that what is being said is not what is really meant? It usually has something to do with the nonverbal messages you are picking up.

Y ou are communicating nonverbally all of the time. To the skilled observer, facial expressions, hand gestures and posture all give away how you are feeling.

Most of the time we are not conscious of the nonverbal messages we are sending and receiving. However, the information is being processed at a subconscious level. It is now well recognized that nonverbal communication influences how we interpret information. When you communicate with others it is less important what you thought you were doing and more important how they interpreted the situation: perception is 100 percent of their reality.

You can increase your personal effectiveness by becoming more aware of unspoken channels of communication.

The importance of appearances

The first element of nonverbal communication is appearance. When you go for a job interview or to an important social event, for example, you will probably take great care about your appearance so that you create a positive impression.

In negotiations you should take equal care. It may help to dress in a way that fits in with the culture of the company or people you are dealing with, whether conservative or relaxed, to create a sense of rapport.

Look out, too, for the signals created by environment. If you are on the other person's territory, what does the environment tell you about their values? If on your own, what does your choice of setting say about you?

Signals to watch

When speaking of body language, we tend to think of posture – things like whether someone sits turned towards or away from the other person.

However, there are a whole range of signals to watch out for. These include eye contact, facial expression and hand gestures as well as posture.

BODY POSTURE

Positive posture is usually relaxed and upright. When they are interested, people tend to lean slightly forward and may cross their legs. When they are less comfortable mentally, people may adopt "closed" postures such as folding their arms or turning their body away from the person who is talking.

When two people are in psychological agreement, this will be reflected in the similarity of body language. This is known as "postural echoing". Look at two friends deep in conversation. Their facial expressions and body positions will be almost like mirror images. When negotiating, look out for signals like these as clues to whether the other party agrees with what you are saying.

Eye contact

Our culture places considerable emphasis on people's ability to make eye contact. It is generally accepted that if someone can't look you in the eye it is because they are lying or in some way uncomfortable with what is being discussed.

Breaking eye contact

Eye contact is believed to be a signal that someone is listening and interested in what is being said. If eye contact is broken for considerable periods of time, it is usually perceived as a signal that the person has lost interest or disagrees with what is being said. If someone you are negotiating with seems to be avoiding eye contact, it may be useful to slow down and spend some time investigating their concerns.

Eye contact as aggression

Although we regard eye contact as a signal of openness and interest, unbroken eye contact is generally perceived to be aggressive or hostile. Psychologists have worked out that the acceptable level of eye contact is around 70 percent!

More eye signals

- If the person breaks eye contact and looks up they are usually thinking – probably considering whether it makes sense or is to their advantage. If they do this, say nothing and let them think about it.
- If they break eye contact and look down, this usually means that they are unsure of, or uncomfortable with, the last thing that was said. You might want to ask what their concern is.

If in doubt, ask

Don't be too mechanistic about reading eye-contact signals, as the same signal can mean very different things in different people or different situations. If you observe a signal that you don't understand, check it out by asking something like "Is there something you are not sure about?" or "Is this still all right with you?"

Most body language is culturally determined and the guidelines given here about eye contact apply mainly to the western cultures. In some other cultures acceptable eye contact levels are much less, and lowering one's eyes is seen as a sign of respect and deference.

THE LIE DETECTOR

It is not uncommon to hear a parent who is trying to get to the bottom of something to say to their child, "Look me in the eye and tell me you didn't do it." This is because it is generally accepted that it is more difficult to lie when looking directly at someone.

Facial expression

After eye contact, the next thing you will tend to notice is someone's facial expression. This is the easiest aspect of body language to interpret; we all know that someone smiles when they are pleased and frowns when they are not.

Use your smile

It may sound like stating the obvious, but your smile is an important tool in dealing with other people. It can create a powerful first impression, sending a signal that you want to be friendly. What's more, if you smile at someone they will tend to smile back. A smile, appropriately used, can often be a way of decreasing tension.

Other common facial expressions

■ The raising or lowering of the eyebrows can mean that the other person has thought of or wants to ask a question.

■ Biting of the lower lip can indicate concern or doubt.

■ Closing the eyes may mean that the other person is trying to shut out other distractions and think about what has just been said.

"Dog-facing"

Some people have very difficult faces to read. This is often referred to as having a deadpan expression or "dog-facing".

Dog-facing is something most people do when they are not thinking about or feeling anything in particular. For instance, you probably do it automatically when you are travelling on public transport, and are not inviting interaction from strangers.

If you have to deal with someone like this it can be extremely unnerving, because nothing that they say seems to be backed up by nonverbal signals. Once you have checked things out with them and they have said that they don't have a problem, you will just have to take their word for it.

Just be sure that you avoid this behaviour yourself. Try to ensure that your face accurately mirrors your thought processes. If you are in agreement, smile and nod to show the other person that you are comfortable with what is happening.

DO YOU LOOK AS FRIENDLY AS YOU FEEL?

Some people have naturally friendly, approachable faces; others seem to wear a perpetually worried or even hostile expression. If you are aware that you tend to look gloomy, make an extra effort to smile periodically and create an open, friendly impression.

Hand gestures

Most people, when they are relaxed and at ease, tend to use their hands to some degree while speaking in order to reinforce their message.

Open gestures are generally thought to imply an open frame of mind. When you are uncomfortable or nervous you will tend to try and control your hands more. This is why, when making business presentations, people often put their hands in their pockets, clasp their hands together or start fidgeting.

Mind your hands

If you know that you are feeling less confident than you would like to appear, make sure that you avoid displaying the gestures that will give you away. If you tend to play with pens, put the pen down. Although you may doodle when you are trying to concentrate, it can also be interpreted as a lack of interest or a sign of arrogance. Remember it's not what you think you are doing that matters – it is how it might be perceived.

"Leakage" is when a person's nonverbal language gives away their true feelings.

THE MEANING OF HAND GESTURES

The following are some typical hand gestures and their possible meanings. Remember that body language may have different meanings from one person to the next, so don't attach too much weight to such gestures.

GESTURE	TYPICAL MEANING
Finger pointing	Aggression/dominance
Rubbing the forehead/temples	Exasperation or defeat
Hands in or near the mouth	Insecurity
Resting side of head in palm	Disagreement or lack of interest
Steepling the hands	Disagreement or lack of interest
Drumming fingers on table	Impatience
Running fingers through hair	Desperation
Hand wringing	Disagreement
Turning ring on finger	Concern
Clicking pen or tapping pen on paper	Impatience
Picking fluff off sleeves	Impatience or disagreement

Using your knowledge of nonverbal signals

Body language is an inexact science, and you should beware of observing a single signal and assuming that it signifies a specific state of mind.

For example, in some accounts of body language you will read that when someone scratches their nose it means that they are lying – however, it might simply mean that they have an itchy nose. Or, you might read that a person rubs the back of their neck to show that you are being a pain in the neck – but it might simply signify that they slept uncomfortably last night.

Making sense of the signals

The way to arrive at an interpretation that is likely to be accurate is to look at what are called "cluster" signals – that is, the combination of different kinds of body language, from eye contact to posture – before drawing your conclusion.

The most important signals in the hierarchy are eye contact and facial expression, so check these first. If they are positive, then a negative signal from, say, posture may be due to the uncomfortable nature of the chairs or the length of the negotiation.

Look out for distinct changes in position – this might indicate a shift mentally and you might want to just check out what is going on in the other person's mind. As you get to know people, look for their patterns of behaviour and pay attention when you notice a change in the pattern.

Watch your language

While you are busy looking at other people's body language, remember that you are sending out signals that will be interpreted by the other party, subconsciously or consciously. You should try to develop an awareness of your own body language. When in discussions, remember to check from time to time that the nonverbal signals you are sending are consistent with your verbal message.

Questioning

The discussion of the negotiation process in Chapter Five has highlighted how important the use of questions is in the art of negotiation. The more questions you ask, the more information you get and the more powerful you can be. Exploring the other party's needs, wants and interests, uncovering any unease that they feel about the deal and gently leading them towards agreement all depend on the skilful use of questions.

What kind of question is that?

A question is not simply a way of eliciting information. It can be used to highlight a doubt or reservation, to get the other person thinking along the lines that you want, or to get the discussion moving faster. There are many different kinds of question, but the two most important categories are open and closed.

Closed questions

A question that can only be answered with "Yes" or "No" is a closed question. Closed questions can be useful for checking your understanding of what has been agreed so far: "So you need delivery within three weeks of placing your order? But you will be able to accept a four-week delivery period on special order items?"

Closed questions can also help to move the discussion on by summarizing what has been said: "Are we agreed on price? Then let's move on to order lead times."

Open questions

Any question that needs a more detailed answer than "Yes" or "No" is an open question. Open questions are intended to obtain specific information, and they begin with the following words:

- why
- who
- what
- when
- where
- how

An open question is often used to explore the answer to a closed question. For example, the question "Are you happy with your present photocopier?", if answered with a "No", is likely to be followed by "What problems do you have with it?"

If you don't ask questions you will be working on assumptions that you haven't bothered to check out.

Remember that to assume can make an ASS of U and ME.

Questioning

Questioning strategies

All questions are either open or closed. But they can be further categorized according to the way they are used. A series of questions can be used to produce a particular response or obtain a particular type of information. Questions can even be used to get the other person thinking differently. The following are all examples of how questions can be used to steer a discussion in a given direction.

Probing questions

This straightforward strategy uses a series of questions to elicit more details about a statement that the other person has made.

Customer:
"I wasn't satisfied with my last supplier."
Supplier:
"What in particular were you dissatisfied about?"
"Can you give me a specific example of a problem you had?"
"How did they deal with the problem?"
"What would you have liked them to do about it?"

Hypothetical questions

In this strategy, questions are used to explore alternatives, to get people to look at the "What ifs?" of a situation. The questions follow an "If…, then…" pattern. For example:
"If we could promise to pay within 30 days, could you agree a discount?"
"If I say yes now, could you start on Monday?"
"Suppose we gave you finished drawings by August instead of just drafts – could you do the costing by early September?"

Defining questions

A series of questions is used to get someone to be more specific about their requirements. Each question is more narrowly focused than the last. For example:
Customer: "I don't like this one."
Supplier: "What is it that you don't like about it?"
Customer: "I don't like the colour."
Supplier: "Would you prefer another shade of yellow, or another colour altogether?"

Intensity questions

In this case, questions are used to investigate the seriousness, or intensity, of a concern that has been expressed by the other person. The effect is to cause them to think again about their objection and perhaps to uncover more of their interests. For example:
Customer: "I wanted delivery by June."
Supplier: "So would a later delivery be no good to you?"
Customer: "Well, it's more a case of building in a safety margin. A later delivery date might be acceptable if you could absolutely guarantee it."

Commitment-building questions

In this strategy, the questions are designed to encourage the other person to increase their level of agreement, and to help you to decide whether they are serious or not. For example:
Customer: "I was really looking for a price about 5 percent lower than that."
Supplier: "So, if I could offer you the lower price, you could go ahead?"
Customer: "I need a delivery by the 14th of the month."

Supplier: "So, if I ring the distribution centre now and confirm that they can meet that date, you will be prepared to sign the agreement?"

Involvement questions

Asking questions that assume the deal has already been made can encourage the other person to think as if it has, and build their commitment.
"So we've agreed on the documentation – this will mean we can start the project next month, doesn't it?"
"So, you'll be able to start doing the internal communication concerning this now, won't you?"

Boomerang questions

A classic strategy for dealing with a difficult question is to answer it with another one:
Customer: "How many colours could you do this in?"
Supplier: "What colours would you like?"
Customer: "How long would it take to put this in place?"
Supplier: "When do you need it by?"

Listening

Keep confirming that
you have understood
the other person with
phrases like:

■ "So what you're
saying is…"
■ "Am I right in
thinking that…"
■ "Then your position
is that…"

Listening is just as important a skill as questioning in negotiations. Your sophisticated questioning techniques can only produce results if you are prepared to listen attentively to the answers.

Take notes

Keeping a note of the key points of a discussion forces you to listen and to summarize what has been said, clarifying anything that you don't understand. It also lets the other person know that you are listening – it is generally accepted that we make a note of things that we regard as important. However, remember that scribbling notes throughout a meeting can make you look as if you are trying to avoid eye contact.

In a long or complicated discussion, make notes especially at points where agreement is reached. This will make it easier to summarize the agreement so far as you approach the close, because you will be able to run quickly through the key points.

Show that you're listening

One of the most irritating things that can happen in a conversation is to get the feeling that the other person just isn't listening to a word. As well as sharpening your listening techniques, take the trouble to show the other person that you really do hear what they're saying.

As well as taking notes, make sure you look as if you are listening. Listening body language includes appropriate eye contact, nodding and leaning forward. It can also be useful to make listening noises such as "uhuh" and "mmm". Beware, however, of the temptation to finish other people's sentences for them. You may think that you're showing you understand what they are saying – they may find it irritating.

SUMMARIZE AND REFLECT

An important technique that you can learn to improve your listening skills and avoid misunderstandings is summarizing and reflecting. When the other person has stated their case, take the key points that have been made and, expressing them as concisely as you can, repeat them back to the speaker. This shows the other person that you have listened to what they said. It is also a useful way of confirming that you have heard what they intended you to hear and, if you have not, gives them a chance to clarify their meaning.

Barriers to listening

You might think that listening is such a basic skill that there shouldn't be any need to learn special techniques. Unfortunately, effective listening isn't always easy in practice. A whole range of barriers can prevent people from hearing what is really being said.

"Dialogue of the deaf"

Often both sides in a discussion are so intent on making their own points that they fail to listen to each other. This is most likely to happen when both sides approach the negotiation with the intention of "winning" rather than reaching mutual agreement.

Experience

In any situation you bring past experience with you. If you have had bad experiences of dealing with a particular company or person or have low expectations of them because of a colleague's opinion, you will not listen receptively to any assurances they give.

Familiarity

When you know someone well you are less likely to listen in detail to what they are saying, mainly because you think you already know what they will say or how they will react. In this situation, you tend to hear what you expect.

Skim listening

Most people are aware that they often skim read – with a newspaper, for example, you look through the headlines and only read those stories that interest you.

A similar process can take place when we listen. We pick up on "trigger" words or phrases – ones that catch our attention – and ignore everything else. If you are the person speaking, you need to anticipate possible trigger words and emphasize them to ensure the attention of the listener.

Attention span

People have limited attention spans – estimates range from 20 minutes to as little as seven minutes. After this, their attention begins to wander. Sometimes the listener's attention is intermittent – they may latch on to something that has been said and go on thinking about it, so that they are not paying attention to the next thing that is said. (This is known as "out listening".)

In any negotiation you need to recognize the fact that attention can drift. Don't let meetings go on for too long – schedule regular breaks. During the meeting, pausing occasionally for interim summaries, making notes and asking questions can all help to keep attention at a higher level.

"Listen, ignore their style, concentrate on the content of what they are saying"

Don't react – respond

When dealing with any situation, you always have a choice of behaviour – you can react or you can respond.

Reacting implies that you have simply followed your impulses. When we react, we often blame other people with self-justifications such as "He made me angry", or "Her behaviour made me feel frustrated."

Responding implies that you have reached a considered decision about what you want to do rather than simply going with your emotional reaction.

An important step in becoming an effective negotiator is to take responsibility for your own behaviour and decide that, no matter what the other person is doing, you will always choose to behave in a mature and professional manner.

Be assertive

When the other party is behaving badly in a discussion, it is easy to become overwhelmed by emotions such as anger, resentment and frustration. Negotiations are rarely successful when emotion has taken over, so you need to develop an assertive way of behaving that will help you to deal with bad behaviour without feeling bullied. Assertiveness can be summarized as:

- saying what you mean
- meaning what you say
- asking for what you want clearly
- listening to what the other person is saying
- being honest about what is relevant
- being prepared to look for a workable compromise.

If you behave assertively, it encourages the other person to do the same.

"Behaviour breeds behaviour"

If someone is angry, they can only keep that emotion going if the other side fuels it. So, by shouting back you encourage the person to shout louder. It will also make them angrier if you tell them not to get angry, or you point out how unreasonable they are being.

Keep the temperature low

If in the negotiating process you observe that either side is becoming emotional, it is always a good idea to suggest a break to allow people to cool off. It is unlikely that problems will be resolved if either or both sides get angry or upset.

Stay detached

If you feel that you cannot take or suggest a break in the proceedings, the best strategy is to remain quiet and let the other person get whatever it is off their chest. People usually run out of steam if there is nothing to fight against. When they have finished you can use the reflecting technique: "I can understand that you are upset about this issue. Let's see what we can do to get around it."

Show respect

When you are dealing with people, it is important that you treat them with respect – even if sometimes you feel they don't deserve it. You can choose to treat someone with respect even if you don't respect them. You can reasonably expect to be treated in the same way. If you adopt an assertive way of conducting your business over time, it is more likely that people will respond in a similar manner.

The standard you should apply to yourself is that you behaved in an adult way, even if the other person didn't. This is especially important if you know you will need to have business dealings with them in the future.

Remember that in any negotiation, whatever the outcome, you are trying to lay the foundations for a long-term relationship in the future. Will your behaviour this time help or hinder you in the future?

THE 4 Ds
In any situation, recognize that you will have at least four possible responses.

- **Deal with it** – if you can't move on until it is settled.
- **Delay dealing with it** – if the other party agrees and delay will not cause a problem.
- **Delegate it** – if you are not the best person to deal with it.
- **Dump it** – if you don't feel strongly about it either way.

7

Recognize game-playing

Empathize

Use time out

Be professional

Why are they saying this now?
What do these figures really mean?
Do I have to decide immediately?

Game-playing

Unfortunately it has become common for people to play games in negotiations, using strategic or psychological tricks to manipulate the other side. This section aims to identify some of the most common games and suggest ways for you to deal with them and minimize their impact.

Game-playing consumes a lot of time and energy on both sides and actually prevents successful outcomes. It inevitably leads to an atmosphere of "point-scoring" and usually distracts attention from the main issues. It also destroys trust between the parties, and damages the possibility of having a long-term relationship.

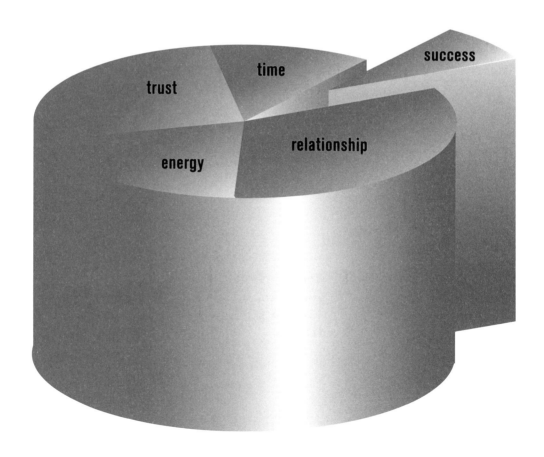

STRATEGY	INTENTION	HOW TO DEAL WITH IT
THE WINCE Someone who doesn't like the position just stated by the other side may respond in an exaggeratedly negative manner – perhaps by using a shocked tone of voice, a sharp intake of breath or a pained expression (or all three).	To make the other side feel that what they have said is unacceptable. The rule seems to be that the person who speaks first once the wince has been played is usually the one to make the concession.	Silence is the best response – most people are uncomfortable with prolonged silence. Make eye contact with the wincer, adopt a neutral facial expression and wait. If this feels uncomfortable, an alternative is to purposefully misinterpret the wince and repeat the statement in a positive way: "Yes, only £5,000".
FRIEND AND FOE You are dealing with more than one person and they seem to be playing opposing roles – one is friendly and conciliatory, the other hostile and uncooperative.	To confuse you and distract you from the business in hand.	Try embarrassing them out of the strategy by pointing out in a friendly tone of voice that you recognize what they are trying to do. Alternatively, check whether the person playing "friend" has the authority to do the deal – if so, then make it clear that you prefer to direct all conversation to them.
THE RED HERRING Towards the end of a negotiation, someone suddenly raises an issue that has not been mentioned before. It is expressed as something which is very important to the deal.	To get more bargaining power by confusing the other side, who thought that the agreement was in its final stages.	Check whether it is a red herring or not. Point out that it hasn't been mentioned earlier and ask whether, if this requirement could not be met, it would mean that agreement could not be reached.

STRATEGY	INTENTION	HOW TO DEAL WITH IT
THE ABSENT OTHER You thought you were dealing with the person who had the authority to make the decision and they suddenly say that they have to consult someone else.	Usually to buy time. The other person may be unsure about a certain element of the deal and want to think more about it.	This may not be a strategy – there really might be someone who has to ratify the agreement. If you think this is the case, ask "Do you feel able to recommend this deal to…?" If they have any reservations this should help to highlight them. Offer to provide any information that they need to "sell" the deal. If you feel that it is a ploy to buy time, ask if there are some parts of the agreement that they would like to clarify. Agree a deadline by which they will let you know the outcome.
FISHING The main deal has been agreed and then the other party asks for something extra, phrased in such a way as to make the request seem minimal. For example, someone has agreed to buy a car and, as the documentation is being agreed, they say that they expect the garage to give them a full tank of petrol.	To get something for nothing. When used effectively this is done in such a low-key, gentle way that the victim thinks that the request is not worth refusing in case it would destroy the rest of the deal.	Decide whether it is worth conceding to the request as a gesture of goodwill. However, you have to assess the real cost of the request, as it may make a difference to your calculations of the value of the deal. If you really object to the request, make it clear that this has not been mentioned before and, while you are prepared to discuss it, it may open up other areas of the agreement for renegotiation.

STRATEGY	INTENTION	HOW TO DEAL WITH IT
PROJECT CREEP This occurs after the agreement has been put in place. The other party then starts to ask for extras which where not included in the original deal. Requests are often opened by "Could you just…?"	To get extra goods or services without additional expenditure.	It is important to nip this in the bud, as once you agree to doing something extra you open the door to future requests, and may end up providing goods or services that you had not taken into account in your original costing. If you have a detailed written agreement, you can draw the other person's attention to the fact that their request lies outside the scope of the contract and that, while you are more than willing to help, it may involve additional costs for them.
BAD BEHAVIOUR One side loses their temper or gets upset. The emotional level of the behaviour is usually out of proportion to the subject matter or situation. They may even get up and leave the room.	To make the other side back down. Most reasonable people when faced with a display of emotion will seek to calm the other person down by making concessions. Generally people will seek to avoid conflict and will look for ways of resolving the problem.	■ Silence – don't fuel the emotion; wait for them to calm down. ■ Suggest time out - five minutes is often enough. ■ Call it – point out that the discussion cannot continue until they calm down. ■ Suggest moving to a less contentious point on the agenda. If the person leaves the room, do not follow them. Wait for them to return when they have calmed down.

STRATEGY	INTENTION	HOW TO DEAL WITH IT
IT'S NOW OR NEVER One person, usually the seller, sets a very tight deadline on the deal. They stress that if a decision is not made now, the cost will go up or the whole deal will have to be renegotiated. They may introduce the deadline when considerable time has already been invested in the negotiation, increasing the pressure on the buyer.	To pressurize the buyer into a quick decision.	You may be able to buy time by saying that, while you have reached agreement in principle, you would like to defer signing the contract for a limited and reasonable time. There are few deals which will disappear completely if you delay your final decision. It is always a good idea to take time out to think a deal through. When under pressure you are unlikely to make the best decision – this is why a "cooling off" period has been built into many contracts that you might sign in everyday life, such as those for financial products or holiday timeshares.
DODGY DENOMINATIONS A large final figure is divided in such a way to make costs look more reasonable. For instance, the other party might divide an an overall cost by the number of employees – "It's £10,000, but to look at it another way, it's only £16 per head".	To make what might be an unacceptable cost sound more reasonable. By referring to what look like reasonable sums of money the other party takes the focus off the real cost.	Keep the focus on the overall figure. Decide whether it represents value for money in the long term, as well as the short. If the final figure is outside your budget, it doesn't matter how it is divided.

STRATEGY	INTENTION	HOW TO DEAL WITH IT
IT'S IN BLACK AND WHITE When discussing price or other requirements, the other party refers to a price list or written specification as the final authority on the matter.	The implication is that because something is printed it is non-negotiable and cannot be discussed. This strategy is designed to curtail any alternative proposals.	Don't be put off by the fact that something is in writing – anything that has been printed can be reprinted. There are very few things that have an absolute value, as prices are set according to certain criteria. Think through how you might alter the criteria. If you have a good rapport with the other person and feel it won't look too confrontational, you could good-humouredly tear up the price list or write down an alternative figure. With a list of criteria, go through it point by point to check whether they are all "must haves" or some of the points can be amended or dropped for the sake of agreement.

Difficult people and situations

People rarely act in a way that is illogical or irrational to them – in their own minds what they are doing makes perfect sense but, because you can't get inside their minds, it may seem very strange to you.

New ways of thinking

It can be frustrating when you have to deal with someone whose approach and attitude doesn't make sense to you, especially if they are also hostile or unpleasant. When negotiating, it is important not to let such frustration get in the way of your goals, so you need to develop strategies for dealing with people who seem difficult.

■ Rule number one, whenever you think that anyone is being unreasonable, is to say to yourself: "They are not being difficult – they are just being different!"

YOUR RIGHTS, MY RIGHTS Do you agree or disagree with the following statements?	AGREE	DISAGREE
I have the right to ask for what I want.		
I have the right to change my mind.		
I have the right to make mistakes.		
I have the right to say "No".		
I have the right to be wrong.		
I have the right to be treated with respect.		

The answer to all of the above questions, for every person, is "Yes", but all of the rights mentioned carry responsibilities and consequences. In addition, if you agree that you have these rights then you should also extend them to the people you deal with. What you might regard as a difficult person or situation is usually due to some confusion surrounding these rights.

- Ask yourself if the other person is deliberately trying to make you angry. If so, realizing this should help you to keep your temper, so their behaviour will not produce the response in you that they intended.
- Remind yourself yourself that they may just be having a bad day – you have no idea what has happened to them prior to your meeting. It is annoying if someone takes out their frustrations out on you just because you happen to be there, but it's not personal!

Learn to empathize

The most common reason for finding someone difficult is that you are seeing things from a different point of view. Psychologists refer to this as "cognitive dissonance" – when two people's ways of viewing the world and thinking about it have little in common. For this reason, one of the most important skills in negotiation is the ability to empathize – to see things from the other's perspective.

Slow down or stop

The main way to deal with this situation is to slow the negotiation process down and spend time identifying areas of mutual interest. It is important to recognize that you do not need to like the people you do business with – you only need to deal with each other in a professional way.

Whatever happens the situation can only be made worse by you losing your temper – using their bad behaviour as an excuse for yours is not very grown up and unlikely to produce effective outcomes. If all else fails, try "time out" – you may be surprised how different something can seem after a break.

No way out

The most difficult situation you can face in negotiations is where you are dealing with a monopoly supplier or customer who is being difficult. Because you do not have alternative suppliers or markets, you will probably develop a fatalistic approach to outcomes. In this case you should concentrate on the relationship and make the process of doing business with each other as easy as possible.

Always remember that the business environment is open to change. New markets can emerge and new businesses open up on a daily basis and one of them could be the new supplier or customer that you are looking for. If you want a more active solution, you might consider expanding your product range so that you are less reliant on a single customer.

How often do you find yourself thinking in the following ways?
- There's just no talking to him.
- She seems determined to create obstacles.
- It's almost as if he doesn't want things to go well.
- How dare she talk to me in that way?
- What's eating him?
- I would rather deal with anyone but her.

CHECKLIST FOR SUCCESS

You know what you want and why it is important.

You are able to prioritize your needs and wants.

You know which issues you are willing to compromise on – if you have to.

You know and understand the limits of your authority.

If you are negotiating as a team you have taken the time to discuss matters so that you have a common understanding and an agreed approach.

You have drawn up an agenda and will open the negotiation by discussing the other person's.

You have researched the people that you will be dealing with.

You have all the information and resources that you might need to refer to during the negotiation.

You have estimated a reasonable time scale for the discussion so that neither you nor they will feel pressurized into a quick decision.

You have considered where the discussion will take place to make both sides as comfortable as possible.

You understand your preferred style of negotiating and its potential strengths and weaknesses.

You recognize the importance of interpersonal skills.

You make sure that your nonverbal communication is consistent with your verbal intentions.

You have a range of questioning strategies that you can use to assist the process.

You understand the importance of active listening and the potential barriers to effective listening.

You know that you have choices in how you behave and are prepared to take responsibility for your actions.

You have identified the non-negotiables that might apply.

You have thought about the areas that might be difficult for the other party and the objections that may need to be overcome.

You have prepared an "escape hatch" that will allow you to leave the door open for future dealings.

You want to achieve WIN:WIN outcomes so that future dealings with the other party will be easier.

You are familiar with the games the other party might play and know how to cope with them.

When faced with problem situations you recognize that people are not being difficult, just different.

Postscript

When you review previous negotiations that you have taken part in, it may be easy to be critical of the outcomes because of information that has since become available or in the light of experience. Don't be too hard on yourself – whatever the situation, people will make the best decision they can with the information available to them at the time. There is little point in saying "If I'd known what I know now…"

The lessons of the past

The real point of reviewing the past is to identify previous mistakes – particularly if you tend to repeat the same kinds of mistakes time and again – and treat them as learning points so that you don't repeat your errors. Negotiating is like any other skill – the more you practise, the more expert you will become.

The skilled negotiator

When you have the opportunity to work with someone who is a skilled negotiator, observe their behaviour. You will probably notice that the secret of their success is the way in which they make it very easy for the other person to agree with them.

The skilled negotiator understands what they can offer that will be a suitable incentive to the other side. They keep their emotions under control and the goal firmly in view, however badly the other behaves.

Most of all they will create an atmosphere of unhurried calm. They don't behave as if they have something to prove. They have sufficient confidence in their own position to be generous in their treatment of others, and they are never afraid to ask questions to increase their level of understanding.

Index